Valentino Assenza

Through Painted Eyes

PIQUANT PRESS

Copyright © Valentino Assenza, 2019

ALL RIGHTS RESERVED. No part of this publication may be reproduced, stored in a retrieval system, or transmitted in any form or by any process – electronic, mechanical, photocopying, recording, or otherwise – without the prior written permission of the copyright owners and Piquant Press. The scanning, uploading and distribution of this via the internet or any other means without the permission of the publisher is illegal and punishable by law. Please purchase only authorized electronic editions, and do not participate in or encourage electronic piracy of copyrighted materials. Your support of the author's rights is appreciated.

Interior design and layout: James Dewar
Cover design: Susan Lynn Reynolds

Author Photo © Richard Glenn Lett
Cover photos courtesy of Big Stock Photo

Published by Piquant Press,
13240 Mast Rd., Port Perry, Ontario, Canada L9L 1B5.
www.piquantpress.ca

ISBN 978-1-927396-13-1 (softcover)
ISBN 978-1-927396-14-8 (e-book)

Earlier versions of the following poems appeared in the following magazines or chapbooks: Don't Look Back, in *Descant #154 (Sicily issue)* October 2011. *The Fan*, *Vignettes*, and The Sower in *Labour Of Love*. Vico Abate and Don Saridu in *Il Ritorno*. Variations In The Sea in *Make Our Peace With Rattlesnakes*.

Printed and bound in Canada

1 2 3 4 5 6 7 8 9 10

For my mother, Joanne Assenza

*"..Chi son? Sono un poeta.
Che cosa faccio? Scrivo.
E come vivo? Vivo.
In povertà mia lieta
scialo da gran signore
rime ed inni damore.
Per sogni e per chimere
e per castelli in aria,
lanima ho milionaria…"*

*"...Who am I? I am a poet.
What do I do? I write.
And how do I live? I live.
In my carefree poverty
I squander rhymes
and love songs like a lord.
When it comes to dreams and visions
and castles in the air,
I've the soul of a millionaire…"*

    –La Boheme, Giacomo Puccini

"…'you know what I think?' she says, 'that people's memories are maybe the fuel they burn to stay alive.'…"

    –After Dark, Haruki Murakami

Acknowledgements

It goes without saying, but thank you to the publishers of this book, Piquant Press. To James Dewar and Sue Reynolds, I extend a huge amount of gratitude, for their enormous support not just with this project, but throughout their years of knowing me. You have always been supportive, enthusiastic, and ultimately with this book, patient, and caring. Indeed, with you, poetry is community and community is poetry. Thank you also to Sonia Di Placido, who contributed with the editing of this book. Another huge debt of gratitude goes out to the mentors I have had in the Toronto poetry community throughout the years. To Norman Cristofoli, for befriending me, first publishing me, and sending me on this beautiful journey of words. To Andrea Thompson, for always assuring me the confidence to be who I am, not just on the page, but also on the stage. Also to the following people who have been both guiding, helpful, and inspiring throughout my years in this community: Rocco De Giacomo, Stephen Humphrey, Jacob Scheier, George Elliott Clarke, Robert Priest, Michael Marian, David Silverberg, Amanda Hiebert, Luciano Iacobelli, Lara Bozabalian, and Nik Beat.

Finally to my family abroad. Simone Assenza and Cristina Assenza. The beginnings of this project all started with our relationship. I am constantly astounded and touched by how amazing you two truly are and how blessed I am that you are in my life. I know our Dad, Giorgio Assenza, is watching. I look forward to the rest of our story, and I'm sure he does too. To my family here in Toronto, my Uncles Michael and Roberto Occhipinti, for always inspiring me to find the rhythm in my words and in my life.

And, of course, to my Mother, Joanne Assenza, to whom this book is dedicated. Thank you for being near a loud typewriter while pregnant with me. Thank you for always including reading and storytelling as part of daily life. And thank you, ultimately, for your unwavering love and support.

Finally, thank you Angela, my love, my heart, and my rock. You taught me that there is a real force in my poetry and always believed in it the way you believed in me.

In your great absence
I've seen this cool crazy life
through these painted eyes.

Table of Contents

Midland
"Remember the Big Wheels on Midland?"

Big Wheels on Midland	1
The Bluffs	3
Mrs. Livia	5
It's Just The Angel's Bowling (Heaven's All Strike Lanes)	11
Butterfly	13

Vico Abate
"From the balcony you could see many other buildings, with windows open, bells from the churches, and the odd ones that rung…"

Campane Di Mattina	16
Dal Balcone	17
Lumache	19
Don't Look Back	23
Vico Abate	27

Bracebridge
"I was tired by summer, looking forward to an Italian summer, went to bed, and turned on the fan…"

The Fan	32
Vignettes	35
Midnight Mass	38
Jack	41
Echo Hill	45
Seven Innings	48

Daleside
"I'll be waiting for you upstairs…"

Daleside	52
Quiet Snow	55
Upstairs	57
Grace and George	62

Corso Umberto
"Io mi metto in piazza e tu mi venga a trovare…"

Don Sarridu	68
U Scapparu	73
The Tobacconist	76
Pomeriggio	83
Blood Orange Sun	85
Variations in the Sea	87

Queen Street East
"You wanted me to see what I had planted…"

Jigsaw	94
Anybody Seen Jimi?	97
The Whistleblower	99
Sky Writing	101
The Sower	104

Midland

"Remember the Big Wheels on Midland?"

Big Wheels on Midland

Every now and again,
one of us says, *Remember big wheels on Midland?*

For both of us,
it's just a miniscule flash
of memory.
One we don't
ever want to lose.

A hot summer day,
our Dads with their shirts off.
Stubbies and 50's beer bottles in their hands.
Talking about things
we didn't understand.

Us passing each other on our big wheels,
exhilaration induced laughter,
being ever so careful
not to ride too close
to traffic.
We were still figuring out all the signals,
Go. Stop. Proceed with caution.

Did we see what was ahead?
Can we trace the trail back
through the blaze?
Parallel paths on a different terrain.
Yours smoothly paved
and mine much rockier.

Who would have thought our big wheels
would have taken us this far?

What ideas did we even have,
other than wanting to be like our Fathers:
upright,
self-assured,
big?

So we rode our big wheels

Today,
the benchmark has aged
but still remains the same.
We stand upright,
continue to
talk about all the things we don't understand
until we ask ourselves,

Remember those big wheels
on Midland?

The Bluffs

South of Saint Augustine's piety,
south of where kids
played chicken.
rebels without causes.
Canadian style
What's a bluff?
They went straight down.
Ok
Is that why they were called bluffs?
Cause they looked like they could have kept going
but then all of a sudden God pulls
the rug from under you?
He was bluffing.

I'm not sure what it is about this place
you liked so much.
Your laughter
associated with this sunny day,
old bread,
and hungry seagulls,
was that all it took?

To make sure I didn't wander off
you held my hand
yours rough and warm,
you once took me
to the edge
your grip was extra hard.
I was scared,
but knew I wouldn't fall.

For Father's Day
and your birthday,
in memory of you,
I will let bread go bad
and after the birds have had their fill
I will leave a single rose behind
Leaving visitors to wonder,
and me to remember.

People tell me that there is a spiritual element
to feeding birds,
especially if you're able
to feed them while in flight.
Is that why you did that?

One hand feeding the birds,
the other holding mine,
and the bluffs in the background.

Mrs. Livia

*"...Aveva una casetta piccolina in Canada
con vasche, pescionlini e tante fiori lili la
e tutte le ragazze che passavono di la
dicevano: che bella la casetta in Canada..."*

Mrs. Livia I can hear your voice,
singing that song,
I can smell your kitchen
you holding me
on top of the table
always smiling
intent
in my eyes
doing your best
to pass on your goodness,
I can understand all
the Italian you spoke
The echo of the words
I spoke back to you
before I spoke a word of English.

Mrs. Livia all I have left
are tiny droplets of memory,
a few pieces missing
from the tapestry
that creates the infant sanctuary
that you cradled
for me
before the two pillars
of mom and dad in my life
would fall away
from themselves.

Mrs. Livia I followed you
to the supermarket,
where you would wait for the train
to cross the bridge every morning,
you'd stop, wait
just so I could wave as it passed,

I followed you everywhere-
to the cemetery,
where I didn't quite understand
why you knelt on the grass
near a headstone,
placed flowers and cried
and into your arms at a running
pace after kindergarten
where you would wait by the
crosswalk with your arms open.

Mrs. Livia sometimes I'm able to close
my eyes
see you knitting in your chair in the basement,
smiling at theme songs from The Waltons,
Happy Days, and Little House On The Prairie.
sometimes if I really concentrate,
I can smell the smoke from your husband Nicolino's pipe,
I can hear his loud voice, and louder laugh,
I can still hear the creek
of the clothes line
as I played in the backyard while
you hung the laundry.
I can still hear the traffic
on Midland, you sitting on your veranda

eating fruit, one of your
favourite past times.

Mrs. Livia I still remember
those moments you comforted me,
how you smiled at me
picking me up and talking to me
in a gentle voice
from the scraped knees
of tricycle accidents
on your driveway
to scratches on my arm
because I didn't know when
to stop leaving your cat Lucy alone,
nowadays in those moments of need
I try to search for that
comforting tone in the wind,
but am rarely able to catch it.

Mrs. Livia,
there is a place in the halls
of sainthood for you,
you foresaw the underrated shadow
over my childhood before I did,
perhaps that's why you called my name
During a stroke so many years later,

I was with you during years
where I didn't know much,
even though there was a day
when your son woke up speaking to you,
and came back unable to talk

and never able to speak again.

Mrs. Livia his silence was your suffering,
a sacred mystery
with your fingers along the prayer
beads of a rosary,
he could only say so much
with hugs, silence and sign language.

But Mrs. Livia, there are children
from that basement,
that are still
coasting with this wheel of life
that you turned for them.
Vince couldn't speak
but they could,
just like I can
just like I do,
My memory banks crying so hard
with my hearts prompt
to pay you the best tribute I possibly can.

Mrs. Livia if your spirit is in the wind,
I have these few words for you,

Che Dio ti benedica
Che Dio ti benedica
Che Dio ti benedica

Mrs. Livia,
all I have left for you
are tiny droplets of memory,

so I wrote this poem
to be back in that basement,
hear you speaking Italian with me,
see you waiting by the crosswalk,
smile at me,
be in your care once again,
if only for a moment.

It's Just the Angels Bowling

Thunderclouds remind me of our living room,
my eyes just above the window sill,
my cautious curiosity,
the sky not so friendly anymore.
I had just finished lunch, but it was getting dark.
Was that a camera flash?
Someone taking
a picture?

The rumble,
eyes closed, make their way
below the window sill
to the vibrating floor.
Rain pelts the awning,
like someone
is tipping
a bucket from the sky
onto the street.

"Don't worry Valentino," my mother says,
"It's just the angel's bowling."

Heaven's all strike lanes,
where perfect games abound
because it's so well lit,
collective halos strategize:
how to give the ball wings.
Each has the magic grip,
without a gutter to spare.

I travel to that uncharted figment,
I figure that's how it must be,

when the rumbles don't stop;
and when I close my eyes,
or cover my ears,
I still feel the rumble.

Year's later,
I'm the kind
who doesn't mind the forecast
when rains parade on,
porches and popcorn,
the darkened skies
—a grey cinespace of dazzling ferocity.

The rumbles continue, small,
miss the streetcar by minutes,
late for work.
Large, making leaps
back and forth on life's libra,
between sadness and guilt,
finding a middle,
gentle balance.

It's late,
I can't sleep.
In my prayers, I ask for thunderclouds,
I ask for someone to turn the lights on.
Heaven's all strike lanes.
I embrace the irony
of how
these rumbles cradle me.
Strength drifts into a dancing calm,
after all, it's just the angel's bowling.

Butterfly

One Day, my Mom handed me a brown paper bag.
"I have a surprise for you, Valentino…"
Inside – I saw delicate, small, multicoloured fans gently waving.
Before I knew they were caterpillars,
I saw this peaceful creature,
doing its best not to be terrified.
What was this beautiful thing? I was captivated.

Before they knew they were caterpillars.
It gently waved its wings, and then it became still.
Was it praying?

Diana the girl next door came over. She was a few years older.
She sat on the veranda with me, curious about my bag.
"It's a butterfly," I said.
She looked at me, "Why isn't it doing anything?"
"It is," I said.
"No it isn't"
I snatched the bag back from her.
Sure enough the butterfly was not moving.

"It's dead," she said.
"No it's not," I objected, not knowing what dead meant.
She raised her voice. "Yes it is. It's dead!"
"No, it's not."
But again, in my head I wondered what dead meant,
not out loud, because I was afraid of the answer.

My Mother heard the commotion from the kitchen.
Through the screen door she soothed, "No Valentino,
she's not dead, she's just sleeping."
I smiled. "See, she's just sleeping."

Diana, defeated, began to walk back to her place.
"See you later."
I watched her leave, sorry to see her go.

Then I looked back at the motionless butterfly.
Still
beautiful.
Still,
and beautiful.

"She's just sleeping," I said.
"She's just sleeping."

Vico Abate

"From the balcony you could see many other buildings, with windows open, bells from the churches, and the odd ones that rung…"

Campane Di Mattina

An open window, an orange groggy sun,
and the bells of Santa Maria,
in a perfect divine madness,
awakening me.

This is no alarm clock.

Chemtrails of jet lag,
remnants of Toronto and Canada linger
as I leave the bed
to look out the window.

Saintly echoes from bell towers.
The boastful vendors
tout below
the greatess of fruits and vegetables
and their low lira cost.

"Bieds fini mille e cinqu o kilu!"

"Citrollu, mille e tri o kilu!"

"Miluna frischu!"

I open the door,
Nonna Carmela waits for me
in the kitchen.

"Buongiorno, hai dormito bene?"

From the Balcony

You could see several buildings,
many open windows, church bells,
some of them ringing.

The legs of the Guerrieri bridge
and the small cars that crossed it
seemed like toys.

This morning I stopped watching cartoons
and wrote another story.
I always asked Dad, "Do you like it?"

It is so hot here.
I wondered about the temperature in Toronto,
how my Mom was doing,
six hours behind,
probably up early, getting ready for work.

After two weeks here, my English
lies buried under one piece of Italian
and another piece of Modicano.

From the balcony
I smell the wonderful tastes,
the anticipation of lunch time,
clear bottles of gassossa,
pasta falling into boiling water.

The music of Claudio Villa
plays from the radio,
and Nonna's birds sing
their own songs.

I wait to see the blue Ford Fiesta.

Soon Dad will be home,
glasses, moustache, and smiles.

From the balcony
I couldn't wait until lunch was done,
waking up from my afternoon nap,
cold espresso.

Tomorrow is Sunday.
We'll speak English,
a word or two that I remember with Dad,
and the Mediterranean will sort everything out.

To this day, I think
I always write for you,
Dad. Do you like it?

Lumache

'After the rain...' says my father.
Scared and impatient,
waiting out a thunder and lightning storm,
I witness the narrow street
under the balcony
swell into a river–
Am I
to become part of a bible story?

Kitchen lights flicker.
A final rumble vibrates my chair,
sky's final scolding
before it calms down
to catch its breath.

The rain follows
as if God
turned down the volume
on water.

Later,
we find ourselves
trudging carefully
through the dark.
He lets me carry the flashlight,
sometimes the bucket–
one hand needs
to be free
to take his hand.

I feel the dry crisp terrain
of the yellow countryside
underneath my wet boots.
I stare out the window

while my hand surfs the wind,
crisped by the extra warm smile
of the sun. After dusk the terrain is dark
and unfamiliar. My father's voice
and the smell of tobacco bring relief.

The flashlight catches stale vines
and long blades of dried grass,
and when he tells me 'slow down'
I see one:
it seems to be an extension
of what it's perched on,
trying it's best to look natural,
but naturally out of place.

The precision of its
circular patterned shell,
delicate movement,
antennae rising,
expressing both curiousity and fear
from being touched.

'Do you want to keep it as a pet?'
Dad jokes.
'What would you name it?'

Clouds unveil
a shower of constellations.
I try my best to search
for a name for this snail,
but the many voices of the
other flashlight folk
distract me.

'I bet we'll get more' I tell him,
We were here before them.

I carry the bucket for a while
Dad is a surgeon with the flashlight
a rhythm between us,
snail shells hitting metal.

Eventually I tell him 'This bucket
is too heavy.'
'I told you,' he says,
but I can't see his irritated face.

It's going to be a long walk
back to the car.

In Nonna Carmela's kitchen,
still night
with flourescent lights,
an open balcony,
telegiornale on TV.

The table holds
casual cutlery
ciabatta buns,
birra
gazzosa
and a bottle opener.

The evening dinner scent of tomato
sauce, capers and garlic—
'Use a toothpick' he tells me.

I look at it

dead, darkened,
I still can't think of a name.
I chew, and swallow, smile, and say
'Sapporito!'
Nonna
smiles back with pride and nods.

As I dunk a piece of bread
into the sauce
I ask my Dad,
'How do you say snails?'
Looking ahead at the TV
—he says 'Lumache.'

'Lumache?' I say, my mouth filled
with sauced bread,

Nonna Carmela says, 'Favalusci,' in Sicilian.

'Lumache' Dad clarifies.
'Lumache,' I say, 'Lumache.'

Don't Look Back

In the bottom of a box
collecting dust
is a tin with a super eight film
of the ceremony.

There is no sound,
except the rotating reels
putting in motion the inevitable.

In front of a gate
with a black car moving through it,

the bride,
the groom,

the two of them hand in hand
looking back at a camera.

It was a sunny day—
no black suit is built
for a Sicilian sun,
even on a wedding day.

Snap!

You could say the picture was iconic.

No need to blink
or time for the eyes to adjust—
the flash was off.

Hold it...just one more!

The photographer had it all wrong—

His pose was to have *i sposi* turn around
looking back.

I would have said:
face forward,
Stand tall,
Stand proud,
Smile—
Don't look back.
There is nothing for you beyond this gate—

A prematurely setting sun;
a palm tree catching
what was left of the breeze;
a man fleeing the country;
a woman sitting on a fence
and a lost little boy
trying to find his way.

The congregation's expression
is consistent
with the weeping angels painted above,
and the Roman soldiers
in the stations of the cross
on the walls.

The mother of the groom
sits stone faced,
the father of the bride
a stern nervousness.
The women fanning themselves
are nearly synchronized,
and the men repeatedly ruin
the flawless white of their handkerchiefs

across their brows.

The bride and groom
have their backs to the camera—
perhaps if they'd turned
around, we'd be able to hear something.

Maybe if they'd faced forward
we'd be able to clearly
hear the priest's words
rather than guess.

Ave Maria.

Maybe if we saw her face,
even through the veil,
we'd be able to make out
the occasional cough
interrupting the benediction

Pieno di grazia.

Maybe if we saw the nervous
squint beneath his glasses
and the half smile beneath
his moustache,
we could hear
uncomfortable shifting
in the cradle of ancient pews.

Il signore e con te.

Instead, during the exchange of vows,
was the ever present vow of silence.

What happened after
The Father, the Son, and the Holy Spirit?
What happened
after the celebratory exodus,
and confetti littering the ancient stone steps?

What happened
after that black car
passed through that gate?

I could tell you,
that the man
found a quiet place to lay low,
but I won't tell you where.

I could tell you
that the woman leapt off the fence,
but I won't tell you which side.

I could tell you
that the lost little boy
found some shade under an olive branch,
but I won't tell you which tree.

What I can tell you is afterwards
the stars shone
and made their mark on the night sky.
After the dawn rose its orange sun
and ignited a new day,
the photographer
took apart his camera and put it in its case—
and eventually they all learned
to face forward.

Vico Abate

I closed my eyes and imagined I was there
remembering the apartment, what it looked like
three years after she died—
nothing more than a scene put on pause.

Her furniture still in its place.
Gassossa still in the fridge
and nothing but a tired moaning,
gust of wind scaring everyone away.

Someone ought to tell them
Nonna Carmela's not returning home.

Her dishes neatly stacked,
pots and pans hung above as if waiting
to place her fine cut garlic cloves
in a frying pan over the gas stove—
break silence in a soothing simmer.

Her bed neatly made, ready to receive her
as if it senses
her homemaking duties wear her down,
help her forget
the tyrannical morning sun of labour
and awaken her
to the relief of a sunken bronze afternoon sun
three hours later.

I can still see Ponte Guerrieri from her balcony.
The towering pillars let everyone know
where the city limits are.
I can still hear the television
endlessly playing her romanzos.

I can still hear the radio, make out the songs,
although they're mostly static.

I can still hear the birds she loved so much,
and her smiles as she mimicked their songs.
I can still hear Tamacun, the puppy on the rooftop,
unaware of the friendship
he would come to have with Dad.

I can still smell the aromas from each room,
the immaculate freshness of the living and dining rooms,
the wondrous smells of the meals
she prepared from the kitchen,
and the smell of the finest bathroom soaps,
courtesy of the tabacchino,
the most distinct being Dad's shaving cream—

I can still see her, Nonna, expressionless,
a consistent, undeniably detailed face—
she never smiled in pictures,
but she sneaked in smiles for her grandson—
a tear escapes as I recall how much of a little shit
I was with her sometimes.

Nonna, I know there was something between us.
Every year when I arrived through the Tabacchino entrance,
I'd say "Permesso" and you, as if on cue,
smiled, always proud proclaiming "Avanti!"

I remember how Dad waited
until she entered her *portone*,
before driving off
a few years later—

I open my eyes,
stand outside Vico Abate,
stare at the doors,
and I wait, I wait until
you are safely inside—
and then I too am on my way.

Bracebridge

"I was tired by summer, looking forward to an Italian summer, went to bed, and turned on the fan…"

The Fan

Lulling liberty,
rhythmic resonance,
shading the circle of silence,
masking it with the onset of serenity.

I tried hard to swim a tenth lap,
sound bites of school vacation screams,
the life guard commands "walk please!"
Waterlog a possibility.
Eleven year-old heart beating rapidly—
I saw them do it on TV,
underwater somersault push off the wall, Damn!

Maybe next time—
depression, distracted by warm sun,
hot dogs, rocks-paper-scissors and ball hockey,

I was tired. I never made that tenth lap,
looking forward to an Italian summer,
went to bed and turned on the fan—
the spinning wheel of relief,
the solemn promise of comfort,
low-medium-high,
choose the setting just after brushing my teeth.

Thirty-six Celsius, humidity is the demon
present, urging me to surrender,
you had me in the balance
who was I kidding—

It was lust,
red hair resilient,
bed of grass,
Cess running through me

like a genie granting me a fourth wish,
but I get high off your skin,
I get high off you letting me in,
lips tasty
Toronto harbour calm.

Sleepy, sweaty,
got up groggy,
turned on the fan.

Electric breeze of bliss,
breeze of a burning relief,
breeze of a mild balance
fulfilling the mood of fantasy.

Carry me away to the places
I have read about in books,
dream about,
and write about.

Mid-January, snow cascading,
below zero
putting me below,
homework interrupted by phone,
message of peace,
message of surrender,
his last breath drawn.

Hospital rendezvous,
family,
tears of sorrow and anger
absorbed by shoulders,
conversation, and funny memories.

Hospital smell gone,
in my bed hoping to dream
and say a proper goodbye,.

Sleep eludes me,
echoes of funeral plans resonate.
Silent sobs lull me, not enough.

Blow out the candle next to his picture,

turn on the fan.

Vignettes

It could have been a little warmer—
I was always reminded of the way
the wind distributed the flakes.
I smiled at the shape
the curtains made as the wind
intruded its way into your bedroom.

Everything outside was non-existent,
including time, or at least I was reassured by the weather
that it would freeze for now.

Your lips were a treat more succulent
than the meal we filled our bellies with.
Pulling you closer,
feeling your body mould to mine,

triggers a flare—

and I suddenly find myself
in my grandmother's basement
with a roaring fire.
She brings me tea and chocolate chip cookies,
the first bite spoiling my dinner.

And there you are,
falling on the bed with me,
eager as can be to take off my sweater.
I find another reason
to hate winter so much
as I fumble about your fabrics.

Skin reveals.
Skin moves.
Skin touches

your skin,
my skin,

triggers a flare—

And I am suddenly on the football field
at my elementary school.
The recess bell as rung,
and I am intent on ringing a young Tony's bell
for attempting to steal one of my X-Men comic books,
two punches in the face.
Knuckle's sore, Mrs. Grieve hauls me away—
no autographs please, my celebrity status
is short lived— once in the principal's office,
in comes the fear.

And there you are—
unhooking your bra was never much of a chore.
Feeling those two beautiful cushions hit my chest
was always an over-pour of excitement.
Feeling your hands initiate their expeditions
and allowing mine to conquer theirs,
presents our sweat.
Your kiss, suddenly harder,

triggers a flare—

And there I am on the calm
of the Mediterranean beach,
the sand veiled by millions of people
engulfed by leisure.
My Dad is intent on outrunning me,
and my nine year-old legs can't keep up.
Lunch time would come.

He liked speaking English with me
and was always curious about
the current Prime Minister.

And there you are—
giving me my a just desserts view,
your smile as beautiful as the moment,
not cold anymore, not cold at all.
When your brown hair throws back,
your eyes close,
my eyes close,

triggers a flare—

And it's my first time
on the Mighty Canadian Minebuster.
My stomach is lost at least four times,
going through that dark tunnel toward the end,
and screaming for no apparent reason,
other than fear of the dark for three seconds,
and I yell and yell and yell,
and I yell and yell and yell—

3 a.m.,
Chinese food containers scatter.
Clothes everywhere but the hamper.
Sheets soaked, window still open,
pneumonia on the way.

Desire is defined,
sentiment is eradicated,
and there I am,
there I am.

Midnight Mass

I can still smell the incense
at twelve.
Pews felt more snug than usual.
Father Mahoney, looking humble as usual,
tries not to rip through the mic, bites his lip,
keeping between his mind and God's,
"Where the hell were you people all year?"

Friends from school with their parents,
even the cool kids, slouch with boredom.
My sweater is itchy.
I avoid scratching.
I roll my eyes at God's routine:

Stand, sit, kneel.
Repeat.

During the Gospel, I stare
at the oversized nativity scene.
My version wants
three wise men
to hold three wizard-wands
with magical powers.

During the homily, I wonder
what I'd get the next morning—
Leafs tickets? A new hockey jersey
to wear during practice?
New games for my Nintendo?
Money?
How much?

I look around and notice families
with dads and siblings,

I keep my composure looking at Mom
her bowed head,
closed eyes.

I wonder what time
dad will call from Italy
in the morning? Maybe we'll talk
for more than ten minutes.

Going up for Communion,
right palm over left,
I'm between looking reverent
and sneaking peeks at Christina.
She sat two desks
in front of me,
hoping she'd notice me
and not the crush
I have on her.

The host on the roof of my mouth is sticky.
This is the part where I am supposed to pray,
my knees on the kneeler.
I do the best I can
to thank God for all the good things.
Bless my family.

"The mass has ended go in the Peace of the Lord."

The congregation is barely able to stay in pews
before the third verse
of "Joy To The World."

One word salutations mimic recess rivals.
Signs of the cross.

Dabs of holy water
and Father Mahoney, with his smiling grey beard,
offers a firm handshake.

People have mixed feelings
about Father Mahoney,
for me, he was one of the few friends I had.

"Merry Christmas, Valentino!
Think the Leafs will do better
in the new year?"

I say yes.
I want to believe.

On the short walk home, through crisp air,
stars peeking out, I wonder, if it was a night like this?
Were the three wizards warm enough in their robes,
carrying gold, frankincense and myrrh?
What was it like on Jesus' second day?

As Mom and I enter the house.
My nose is filled with the smell of pine.
I keep hopeful for a short sleep
and a Christmas morning
with majestic icicles.

Jack

Cuts hair.
He wears striped shirts,
black dress pants
and glasses that he lets slide down
to the end of his nose.
Jack cuts hair.
His Barbershop is littered with antiques, old saws, spittoons,
cameras, canes, and canisters.
A sign says "Complaint Department, take a number."
The number itself is attached
to the pin of a grenade

His Barbershop
is by a street light.
People look in the window,
see you getting your haircut.
From their cars they laugh
or make ghastly facial expressions.
Jack sometimes glances
back at them and waves.

With his handy work,
he can tell what kind of day
they're having.

My first haircut when I was
ten years old,
Summer of '85, acquainted with my new digs.
Finishing off a blue freezie
after a swim at the local pool.
Jack folded the blanket
over his left arm
and said "next victim." He looked directly at me.

Jack cuts hair
I sit in his antique
barber's chair,
with cow-patterned leather seats.
Jack never asks how I want it.
He's got it down to an exact science,
or rather less than exact science.

He takes a number one
more often than not
decimates the out of control 'fro
that grows it's way atop my head.
When he's finished trimming
my sideburns, back burns,
and other assorted touch ups,
he takes off the overgrown bib.
I look in the mirror
ready to enlist.

Jack asks me
how my life is going
I tell him that I'm taking
as many punches as I can,
trying to punch back
just as hard.
Jack tells me to punch back harder.

My girlfriend doesn't like
Jack's haircuts.
She suggests I got to a stylist—
I've tried.
I cheated on Jack twice—
Once going to a queer, but gay, biker.
and once I went to a place where they asked,

"Would you like a cappuccino, or a latte?"
while washing my hair.
The cuts were great, but they weren't Jack.

Jack cuts hair.
Jack tells stories,
gives advice.
Jack always says I should
listen to Mom. He thinks
I should lose weight—
he doesn't want me
to die of a heart attack,
he doesn't want me to die alone.
Jack's wife died of cancer.
He remarried. He says, "You should get married."
Jack thinks I'm a good guy
with a good head on my shoulders.
He doesn't think any man is an island.

Jack entertains the East York elderly
with jokes as old as them.
Jack makes himself a tea in the back,
flips on the CD player, listens
to Celtic and Maritime music.
Jack reads the Toronto Star.
He never discusses his politics.
Jack's a world traveler-
twice a year the barbershop closes.
He's likely on a Norwegian Cruise
dazzling some lady at the bar
with some beautiful barbershop blather.

Jack cuts hair.
He takes the place of a shrink,

he'll never steer you wrong.
With scissors in hand, he snips away
or brushes the hair from you-
Jack knows things about your life
that you couldn't know,
but would you have it any other way?

Jack cuts hair.
I tell him to keep five.
He tells me, "Much appreciated, take care now."
I leave Jack's barbershop,
look back at the window,
see the scattered array of artifacts.
The next victim arrives,
completes the picture
sits in Jack's chair.

Echo Hill

Blaise looked at me, *"You know why they call it Echo Hill?"*

He screamed, *"Hello!"*
Like a slingshot, his voice greeted us back,
bouncing off seniors' homes and the barren trees
of Taylor Massey Creek below.

I decided to do the same, admire
the sound of my voice in the air
on our old tobogganing haunt.

We were careful to ride our bikes down
this steep hill in summer
with our hands cautious on the breaks.

But these snowfalls, we waited for—
the ones worth packing,
The ones worth serving up
with spherical splendor,
and the ones worth
going down Echo Hill

The exhilaration
of going fast,
but not too far, not down into the creek,
No, not into the creek.

In the summer
it was a haven for exploration.
We're on our bikes, fierce road warriors,
explorers, hoping to encounter
a Stephen King circumstance—
a pond full of leeches,
or a cave where we had to give

each other courage before entering,
regardless of the season.
That was us: trying to find
the best way to get lost.

But in winter,
Taylor Massey Creek was the ultimate void.
Maybe our adrenaline hid there,
beyond what we didn't know,
beyond what we didn't know.

It was this downhill slide,
followed by the uphill climb,
that was worth it—
repeat—
the downhill slide
followed by an uphill climb,
that was worth it.

It was the comfort
of the afternoon sun,
escape from Saturday morning cartoons.
Before the hot chocolate by a woodstove,
and Hockey Night In Canada.
Before the dreary Sunday hours elapsed
so much quicker, compressing the cram
of homework— that annoying voice
only we could hear, that kept telling us:
school is tomorrow,
school is tomorrow.

We didn't want to hear school is tomorrow.
We wanted to catch a detailed snowflake
in our mouths, wanted a downhill slide,

followed by an uphill climb
that was worth catching our breath—

At the top we scream *Hello!*
Greeted by ourselves
time and time again.

Seven Innings

For my cousin Giorgio Occhipinti

Top of the first,
first things first—
a message on the answering machine,
you telling me to bring my glove
and a Louisville Slugger state of mind—

There's an empty schoolyard
with an almost perfect square
spray-painted on the wall.
A strike zone just above the knees,
and below the elbows.

What exactly is the basis of running bases?
Let's just set a boundary, single, double, triple,
then a home run—
we always swing for the fences.

Bottom of the second,
second as in two, like we two,
and two and two is four,
and you're four years younger than me,
but I'm scared of you.
Two as in two outs, no fuss no muss.
The ball bounces right back to you,
off the wall, but harder to bluff.
Harder to talk one game,
throw a curve with another,

It's a nice day. The wind's blowing toward the fences.

Middle of the third,
we drink Gatorade, wear batting gloves,
let Big League Chew juice spill

from our mouths to the pavement,
cause we're cool—I said we're cool—
who cares if no one's here to see?
We're cool. "Ball's in, coming down!"
And we're still aiming for the fences.

Bottom of the fourth,
and we have this weird obsession
with Bill Murray. He's a Mets' fan—
while we're fetching balls, throwing warm-ups,
and perfecting practice swings,
we're trading quotes from "What About Bob"
and "Groundhog Day" reiterating baby steps
and Punxsutawney Phil.

We can go to Warden Woods, watch a movie,
play some video games, is there anything else to do
in that mall anyway— and then you throw a strike,
my third, catch me looking.
I'm still nowhere near those fences.

Top of the 5th,
and a swing, a miss, a swing, a miss.
You ain't gettin' that cheese by me meat.
I'm your older cousin. I'm a wannabe Crash Davis.
I'm a Robert Redford armed with a thunderbolt.
I'm Shoeless Joe walking out of the cornfield.
Just put it low and away. I dare you.

You're just a kid—
I buy you caramel corn. I take you to the movies
and Jays' games where we rise to our feet
with the rest of the crowd,

when the ball is hit
deep toward the fences.

The sixth inning already?
Why do these days end so quickly?
What do we want to be when we grow up?
Full count, three and two—
sometimes you settle for a base hit,
take a strikeout like a man,
or cry foul, but eventually you run out of chances.
In my head, I point to the left field fences.

Then we'll find a way
to make this seventh inning stretch,
that superhuman dive for an out,
arguing whether the ball was in the box,
arms tired from throwing so many k's
eternally searching for KO'S.

We squeeze every ounce from this two-man
makeshift baseball game we call burby,
not really noticing the ghost of a run batted in,
leading off at second, ready for the spring
in his step to sprout— perhaps he blew that gust of wind
that leaves the ball briefly dancing on the air,
only to pause long enough for a crack of the bat—
the two of us looking skyward, one smile, one frown,
overturned faces watching gravity at its finest.

Daleside

"I'll be waiting for you upstairs…"

Daleside

I don't know why
I keep dreaming about that house—

There's a part of me
that doesn't want to leave.

I can still hear her voice
on the answering machine
in her broken English
"Hi Valentino, are you back home from school?
would you like to come over,
rake the leaves?
You can do your homework here
I'll make you something to eat."

I never minded.

Those days would often end
with me in the basement family room,
falling asleep to the smell of a fireplace
and the sound of "Wheel Of Fortune" on television.

I remember the street,
the crescent, almost zero traffic,
where I learned to ride a bike,
and where most street hockey games
almost never needed the word "car!"

I remember the kitchen,
how the morning light shone through,
and how grandma always
sat at the table for breakfast
with a half grapefruit.

I remember the living room
the same one where my grandfather
tried to surprise my grandmother
with an accordion he got for a job instead of money—
But instead, half scared her
that an intruder had entered
as a horrible sound emanated
confirming he couldn't play it at all.

Sundays family full, bottles of mineral water,
and homemade red wine,
Cavatiedi, ravioli, and sauce never duplicated,
loud intercutting conversation.

I remember sick days from school in the TV room,
"The Price Is Right" and Macdonald Carey always saying,
"These are the days of our lives."

I remember the gas powered lawn mower,
that I always yanked at so hard
afraid the motor would actually start
The garage, the myriad of Grandpa's tools
how did he ever find anything?
There was a method to that madness.

The backyard,
the oldest rudimentary hibachi grill,
that made the meat taste that much better.
The picnic table made from a highway sign.
We ate food just above where it told you
how many kilometers to go to Tweed.
A train would always pass by,
and I would always laugh at the word "caboose."

The basement,
the scary temple of doom
laundry and furnace room,
the cantina, demijans emanating
the smells of both aged and old wine.

In my dreams,
I can still here her voice throughout the hall,
"Valentinuzzo gioia veni ca"
I can still hear old Julio Iglesias songs on the stereo,
the sounds of a game show on the television—

In the warm smell of the fireplace,
I fall asleep on the couch.

Quiet Snow

The night he died,
I noticed
just how silent, and peaceful
gentle snowfalls can be
I should have
stayed in front of our house,
on our small deserted street,
followed
the whispering cascade of flakes.
against the black of the sky,
to the orange glow of the street lamp—

found the asphalt
where the finality of a flake rests,
but a second,
then melts away.

On one particular night,
company had come over,
family and many friends,
in his crowded, loud house.
At one point I noticed
that he wasn't there,
I went to the backyard,
a bit scared
because it was dark.
When I saw him, I was relieved.

He leaned against the brick wall
looking at a freight train passing
behind the football field.

I tried to sneak up on him
but he noticed right away.

"Nonno," I asked
"What are you doing out here?"
He looked back out into the yard.
"It's quiet."
"It's quiet?" I asked.
"Listen, see? It's quiet."

That January night
I came into my house
after getting the phone call, "He's gone."
I now realize
maybe that's what he
was looking for—quiet.

Perhaps the confinement of a hospital bed,
where a once enthusiastic voice struggled to speak,
subsequent strokes stinting at certain parts,
that once helped build indestructible structures,
perhaps that made too much noise.

That night, an old record player
suddenly played Rugantino
in perfect harmony
"Roma nun 'fa la stupida sta sera"

The next morning gentle
flakes collected on the ground
You stood in front of the yard
with a white suit and a blue handkerchief
in your left breast pocket;
behind you in the garden, through the snow,
grew a single red rose,
"Nonno, what are you doing out here?"
"It's quiet."

Upstairs

He's waiting for me
upstairs
in the bedroom.
It's the reason
why the thermostat
isn't making much
of a difference.
It's the reason
why I keep hearing
a vibrating noise
and no one else does,
and why I'm that much
closer to tears—I know
the only way
to make that
vibrating noise stop.

He's waiting for me
upstairs,
and I'm trying to focus
my eyes on the
finer details,
like an empty stained
espresso cup,
my wife
wiping her brow
as she yawns,
and that pattern
on the kitchen tiles.

But he's waiting for me
upstairs,
and I don't want to go.
It's why I hold her

waist a little tighter,
why my lips stick
to her cheek a little longer,
and why I linger
for a few seconds more
after "goodnight"...
"Buona notte.."

And I'll get to the top
of these stairs
and look back once more,
catching the light from the
kitchen and the muffled sounds
from the television.
And I'll enter that room
that's colder than most
and his hand will be there.
Only a few seconds will pass
before I take it.

And so I'll be taken
over seven decades,
dispelled in a wink
with the whisper of
life's sands slipping away.
My eyes will be closed
by grace,
my body felled
by the turn
of this life's chapter.
I'll be treated
to a final once around
that exists on the multicoloured
collage that makes up

my life,
that precious
subliminal taste
of the past through
my senses.

The sight
of the endless
Mediterranean in the afternoon,
my father peeling
me a cucumber from
the garden,
and a lizard
crawling across a stone wall.
The smells of jasmine
outside my house
the day I left my homeland,
tomato sauce on a stove
so good I want to break
a piece of bread off
and dip it in the pan.
The taste
of bread,
cheese and olives
in my mouth
at the same time,
chased with my
own painstaking
homemade wine.

The feel
of her hand first
brushing mine
and my body

first brushing hers.
The sounds
of my daughter's first
cries.
The scattered laughter
of my grandchildren,
clamour and banter
at the dinner table
totaling to Pavarotti
in Tosca
singing:
"L'ora e fuggita,
e muoio disperato
e muuoio disperato..."

And then the fog
will part,
and the dust will
settle
and I'll
pass through
two endless pillars
and the white
threshold that
snaps like thunder,
only to be halted
by St. Peter's staff.
But you my love,
you'll wipe your tears,
and days will pass
with you in the garden
mending fallen flowers,
grandchildren
on your lap

looking up at you
with regal admiration.

Eventually you won't wear black anymore.
You'll get the hang of days again.
Laughing at jokes
will come a little easier.
You'll take sunny,
dewy, early morning
walks.
You'll be a walking
definition for pride.
One day,
maybe not so soon,
you'll come home
one night,
and make yourself an espresso stretto.

The thermostat
won't work like it's
supposed to.
You'll hear that same
vibration coming
from the coldest
room in the house—don't be alarmed
my love—leave the dishes in the sink,
turn off the television.
No need for panic my love.
It will just be me
with my hand out,
waiting for you
upstairs.

Grace and George

My Mom tells me the story of how my grandfather courted my grandmother.

He walked many kilometers to my Zia Sarrida's house to see her. He walked right up to the door, knocked on it and said, *"Vuogghiu virri Razzietta!"*

And my Zia Sarrida, making bread with my grandmother and her friend, didn't even bother getting up to come the door. She responded, *"Vattini a casa! Chistu non mi piaci, siemu tri fiminedi chi stam facienu u pani, lassa stari."*

He was told, before walking back all those other kilometers, that he could only try so many more times.

But of course he kept trying. *"Vuogghiu virri Razzietta."*

Grace met George through her Maestra, who taught her sewing. She had a gramophone, and always invited people over. That is when George first caught Grace's eye. *"Vuogghiu virri Razzietta."*

"Vattini a casa tadiu rittu!"

Of course they were able to figure out a way to see each other outside of the supervision of my Zia Sarrida, and eventually dating turned to marriage, and marriage delivered two children, Jo-Anne and Peter. The war had just ended and they searched for new horizons. Sicily was getting tired, so they aimed elsewhere, across the ocean to Canada, Toronto, Canada.

"Vuogghiu virri Razzietta"

"Buonu ciui, tadiu rittu, siemu tri fiminedi che stamu facienu u pani, vattini a casa!"

They travelled across the ocean separately. George came first. Grace followed later with Joanne and Peter. My Mom tells me about arriving at Pier 21, and the train ride from Halifax to Toronto. She tells me about how soft the Wonder bread felt. The bread was so soft that they would roll it up into balls and throw it at each other to pass the time on the train. She tells me about arriving in Toronto, how Grace, Joanne, and Peter, met up with George and Uncle Jim at Union Station. While in the car on their way to a rooming house on Berkeley Street, they became so excited to see one another that they talked frantically in Italian. Uncle Jim turned to them and said, "You're in Canada, now. You speak English."

"Vuogghiu virri Razzietta."

"A finiscacilla!"

George and his brother Joe were stonemasons. They found enough work to make their way out of the Berkeley street rooming house and move to the east end on Amroth. They didn't need phones. Joe and Tony, George's brothers, lived nearby. All they had to do was open a window and call out.

"Vuogghiu virri Razietta!"

"A zittiti pi piaciri!"

Soon they moved to Glenmount. Grace and George needed help. Robert and Sylvia had arrived, and Joanne had to drop out of school. Joanne occupied them all, whether it was letting go of Sylvia's pram down the steephill on Glenmount, or taking them all out to see "To Kill a Mockingbird" at the Prince Of Wales theater. They had a pet rabbit that one day ran away. However, one night seated around the dinner table, Joanne asked, "What's for dinner?" and George responded with, "We're having chicken."

"Vuogghiu virri Razzietta!"

"Vattini a casa!"

By the time they got to Daleside, Michael had arrived, and Grace and George now had five kids. They had settled in to life in Canada well. Grace and George loved to entertain, hosting big family Sunday dinners, and sometimes picnics at Musselman's lake. They sent the relatives back home pictures with lots of bottles on the table, or someone talking on the telephone.

Vuogghiu virri Razietta!"

"Canta na canzuna!"

In addition to smoking Export A cigarettes, drinking stubbie bottles of 50, and homemade wine, George loved to sing. He loved music. He used to be part of a band in Sicily. Often times when he walked into a silent room, the first thing he asked, "Uni e a musica?!" You would often hear him listening to, and sometimes singing along with operas like Tosca, and Rugantino. He especially loved the songs of Claudio Villa.

"Vuogghiu virri Razietta!"

"Lassa stari nun ti fazzu trasiri!"

They were known to many of their Canadian friends as Grace and George, but I came to know them as my grandparents. I always felt close to my grandmother Grace. I was her eldest nephew, but since I had been to Sicily, I was able to speak Sicilian with her. I felt the same closeness with my grandfather. I'm still charmed by little memories, between the two of them, like Grace asking George if he washed his hands before dinner, and my grandfather just casually saying "Puliti su!"

"Vuogghiu virri Razzietta!"

My grandfather worked so hard all of his life, but when he retired he was rewarded with Parkinson's and strokes. He died at 70. He went first this time. Grace followed him two years later with strokes of her own.

"Vuogghiu virri Razietta!"

Grace and George. Giorgio and Orazia. Razzietta e Giuginu. They decided to cross the ocean one day to give a better life to us. Look back and see these beautiful colours, how they connect these tapestries we want to hold onto or uncover for ourselves. These precious increments of memory that we want to burn: Grace and George.

"Vuogghiu virri Razietta"

When I go to the cemetery I wonder where they are now. I look at the headstone and part of me wonders if they are that age all over again. Grace is at Zia Sarrida's house sitting down making bread and George comes calling.

"Vuogghiu virri Razzietta!"

But this time, Zia Sarrida comes to the door, opens it, smiles and says: *"Entra, si accomoda."*

Corso Umberto

"Io mi metto in piazza e tu mi venga a trovare…"

Don Sarridu

For a short while, my father owned a trattoria. I remember how the trattoria was run so much differently than a restaurant here in Toronto. For instance, there was no menu. My stepmother would cook a bunch of food, and when the lunch rush came, they would just casually ask what was available to eat and order what they wanted.

They did not have a wine list; it was either "vino rosso" or "vino bianco." It would be ordered by the litre or half litre. Sometimes I would find myself under a demijan carefully opening a litre of red.

Much like my father's tabacchino, what I liked most about the trattoria was the clientele. Modica is a city that actually attracts quite a few tourists, it has such a character, and it is near some of the most beautiful beaches in Sicily. The people in the trattoria would either be European tourists, or they would be older men. I was always fascinated and entertained because they yelled all the time. And as vino rosso entered their system they became progressively louder.

What fascinated me as a kid was how they addressed each other. "O Don Pietru, comu si?" Or "O Don Pippinu chi si dici?" This was where I was first introduced to the whole concept of "Don."

Everyone spoke Modicano, or Sicilian. I rarely heard someone speak textbook Italian. Putting "Don" in front of a name mimicked the priesthood. When you addressed a priest as "Don" it would be a form of respect, and the older men followed the same protocol.

It was during this period that I spent in the Trattoria that I met Don Sarridu. Sarridu is the Sicilian variation of the name Rosario. Don Saridu was among many friends in the trattoria. He sold fruit and vegetables for a living. Don Sarridu drove an "Ape", a small truck vendors drove to sell their produce. Translated it means bee. If you lived in a neighbourhood where Don Sarridu worked you would not need an alarm because at around 7:30 am he would be outside your house in your neighbourhood yelling "pumadoro mille e cingu o kilu, citrollu due milla lira," Without fail, early in the morning, he would be there with all of the other Ape vendors. I'd always recognize his yelling voice when he entered the trattoria because I heard him selling fruits and vegetables on the street.

Don Sarridu always attempted to speak English with me. My Dad told me that for a short period of time he lived in Connecticut. He spoke English but it was very broken. He would mention a couple of things like James Brown, and baseball, and he would get excited about certain subjects. When he got really excited he talked faster and faster until I wasn't able to understand him. To save face he would change the subject to Sicilian. He would always order a little wine for himself. And it's funny but the more he drank, the better his English got.

He would always offer me food when he was sitting playing cards with his other friends. He took a great liking to me and was always curious about my life in Canada.

I always looked forward to him coming through the door and everyone yelling "O Don Sarridu!" myself included.

He would always turn to me jokingly and say, "Valentino, red wine please?"

It so happened one night, after my Dad closed the trattoria, he went to pick up my grandmother Nonna Carmela. She helped look after the Tabacchino, and needed a drive home. On this one particular night en route to Nonna Carmela's house, my Dad was only minutes away from dropping off my grandmother when he stopped the car. My Dad bent his head down and looked out the windshield.

"Ma pichi ni fermamu?" my grandmother asked. "Why are we stopping?"

I was also curious and my Dad turned and looked at me. "Look out your window," he said, "look up there."

I looked out the window and saw a smaller road fork upward and at the top of this road was a small building with a solitary balcony, a room with a light on, and the silhouette of someone with his arms hanging over the balcony.

"You know who that is?" My Dad said to me. I shrugged.

He smiled and said "That's Don Sarridu."

I didn't believe him.

But my Dad said, "Go ahead, call to him."

Not believing my Dad, but being hopeful, I stuck my head out of his blue Ford Fiesta and in my loudest voice yelled "Don Saridu!"

Dad wasn't pulling my chain, almost instantaneously in his best vendor voice he yelled back, "O Valentino!"

My Dad started driving and we all laughed uncontrollably in the car.

Since my Dad followed, basically the same routine during the week, I came with him on all the rides, and sure enough Don Sarridu would be out on the balcony, and it became part of the routine.

I'd spot him smoking his cigarette on the balcony. My Dad would stop the car, and soon after would follow the exchange. "Don Sarridu!"

And he would shoot back, "O Valentino!"

This soon became a bragging right for me. I would tell all my friends in Modica about what would happen with my Dad, and funny enough they were that jealous that they tried the same thing. Don Sarridu however proved to me that it was all a respect thing for me. This was his way of calling me "Don." He would only call back specifically to me.

Other kids would see him at night and call out "O Don Sarridu!"

And he would yell back, "Zittitti ca ci sunu persuni che stannu durmienu!" meaning, "Shut up! People are trying to sleep!"

Summer would end and I would soon head back to school and

Canadian winter.

The night before I left to go back to Toronto, I passed his balcony one more time. I yelled out "Ne vediemu Don Saridu!" letting him know, I'll see you later.

He returned with, "O Valentino, fai nu buon viaddiu" meaning "Have a good trip."

During the time that I was in Toronto, whenever I talked to my Dad he would always tell me that Don Sarridu asked about me. Towards next summer though, my Dad informed me that he believed Don Sarridu was ill because he stopped coming to the restaurant. People began to worry that he was not well.

That following summer when we returned to Sicily, I never saw him at all in Trattoria. My Dad still followed the same route to drive my grandmother home, but when I looked up at Don Sarridu's balcony, it was repeatedly empty. But one night, towards the end of the summer, we drove by his house and he was there. He stood in his famous silhouette pose. I was so excited that my Dad stopped the car. I yelled out "Don Sarridu!" as loudly as I could.

After a pause, his head looked up. I heard a few coughs, and in a tired, grumbling voice I heard, "O Valentino!" He made himself heard, but his vendor voice was gone.

We returned to Toronto and later that year my Dad called to inform me that Don Sarridu had passed away. I only knew him from seeing him in the Trattoria, and yelling up at him when he was on his balcony, but I still felt sad.

Many years passed. My Dad closed the Trattoria. My grandmother passed away. I turned into a teenager. The young girls I had been friends with as a kid had grown up and become beautiful women. They became my distraction.

One day I went riding on my vespa with my friend Francesco. I followed him and he took the same route we used to take to drop off my grandmother. We passed by Don Sarridu's house and the balcony was not only empty, but the green shutters had been closed tight.

In my loudest voice I yelled, "Don Sarridu!"

Francesco looked back at me as though I'd lost my mind. I laughed at the expression on his face.

And I laughed again when I thought I heard Don Sarridu calling back, "O Valentino!"

U Scapparu

La Zoccola also called Ciabatta,
much like an in-house slipper,
for the moments of having just cleaned
"Ho gia pulito."
Watching soap operas in groups,
and doing crosswords
at the kitchen table,
while stove smells increase your hunger.

The Sandal,
for scorched toes in scalding sand,
to be removed before sampling
the temperature of the Mediterranean,
to trap sand while walking the desert,
to walk miles before greeting John The Baptist,
and taking his hand.

The Loafer
The one that makes you walk slower
because you really don't want to be there.
It's uncomfortable,
so you lean on whatever you can,
you sit on any chair available,
for breaks, lunches and casting aside
when you arrive home.

The Runner or the Sneaker
"La Scarpa Di Ginastica"
For running with the hunted,
for making sport of the sporadic,
for moments of "calcio di rigore"
and relay races
where you're never the anchor
but constantly passing the baton.

The Dress Shoes
The ones you polished
ever so rigorously,
the ones you stare at
in the reflection of the mirror
perfecting the precision knot of your cravat.
The ones that make you
put your blazer on
with the emphasis of an emperor.
The ones that announce
your presence with authority,
tap tap tapping the tapestry
of your life's new beginning.
You hope that shine catches her eye
from across the room.

The High Heel
Tacco Alto,
Harder to dance in, let alone walk.
Best to have the arm of a gentleman
to break the fall in love
pump, peep toe, who really notices?
Or if the occasion should strike
there could be the sauciness
of a succubus in a short skirt
and the impetus to follow the trail.
The cohesive curvature,
the smooth sullen segue of her leg,
perfect for drunken durges in a courtyard on mandolin.
For leaning back on
the inebriated confidence of deep glasses of red,
and he had just as many,
but notices, as he places the anklet on you
just above your right foot.

Notices the steps echoing
off late night dormant buildings,
the echoes of the steps from your stairwell.
Notices when he bends over
and you lean on his shoulder
so he can take one shoe off. He notices.

U Scapparu
The Shoemaker
The Cobbler
Lo conosci?
Do you know him?
Everyone knows him.
He has a moustache,
"ci piace giocare a carte,"
carries a scented name,
a gentleman, has a wife and two children,
rolls his own cigarettes,
takes his hat off whenever he enters a room,
offers a firm handshake.
Do you know him? Everyone knows him.
What shoes does he wear?

The Tobacconist

I'm leaning my elbows
on the counter.

Not because
I'm feeling lazy,
and not because
I'm trying to emulate
his picture on the
wall of cigarettes
behind me.

It's easier
to eat pistachios
this way.
I'm nearing a hundred—
there's a nice
little mound of shells
that make me feel proud.

It's a hot day,
it's nice to have
a lull.

Pretty soon
that beaded entrance
will be divided,
and someone
will come through
and say "permesso,"
and I will say
"avanti."

The sign on the front
window says:

"Come in, we speak English"
but they don't.

I'll be at the ready
to grasp their
flavour of nicotine.
Whatever brand waits
at the tip
of their jonesing tongue,
I can find with my eyes closed.

"MS dure."
"Un pacu di Merit."
"Lucky Strike senza filtru."
"Un pacu di Marlboro Lights pi piaciri."

Sometimes,
that'll be it,
an exchange of
one word pleasantries
and Lights for Lira.

Other times,
they'll let me know
that I'm more to them
than a peddler.

Stay for awhile.
I'll smoke with you.
My brand is Rothman's.
These things will be
the death of me,
but in the meantime,
let me put one in

my mouth
and let me suck
back the flame
so we can
ignite some conversation.

I'll ask a question
and you serve me
some horse shit—
let's blow smoke
while we blow smoke.

'Cause that's
what it usually is,
horse shit,
and I'll take
any brand of that,
littered
with the finest
of Modicano swearing.

"stu fidiu ri butana
 mi rubao i soldi."
"Minghia ra veru?"

Come on, Turidu,
roll one for yourself
and tell us
about the time
you hitched a ride
to Marina
and the guy
in the car
tried to grab your balls.

Cicciu.
Let a Marlboro
hang from your mouth,
and tell us about
how you gave the captain
a big wheel of cheese
to keep your son
from being drafted
by the army.

Sprinkle some tobacco
on your pipe, Pippinu,
and tell us
about the bet
Queen Elizabeth I
made with Sir Walter Raleigh
over the fact that
smoke can be weighed.
The Queen enjoys a stogie?
Man, that's heavy.

I didn't grow
to be an old man—
my smile
and penchant for
laughter and horseshit
keep me from it.

But I come back
once in awhile,

and occasionally
I here the echoes
of smoke

that were once
blown here.

Sometimes,
I still taste
the Latte Di Mandorla
that I would have
with my fringozze
in the morning
while listening to the news on the radio.

Sometimes,
I'm right back there
with my elbows
on the counter
in a t-shirt,
levi's jeans
and Addidas running shoes.

They'd see me,
I'd see them.
The regulars,
their brands of cigarettes
and horse shit,
friends,
with invitations
to dinner in the country,
so we can eat too much meat,
drink too much wine,
and the tourists
never to be seen again.

If I got thirsty,
I'd go to the bar

next door and get myself
a Nastro Azzuro.
If I got bored
I'd read Time magazine
to keep up my English.
And if I got tired,
I closed.

So let me close
tonight.

Just one more time.

I remember how it's done.

One final sweep
of the floor,
a flash of memory—
my mother seated in that chair
by the cash register.

One final printout
on the till
and I think about
your wife waiting
at home for you.

Before locking the door
I change the sign
from "Aperto" to "Chiuso"

I can still
feel the weight
of that giant lock,

the one you'd
put to secure
that big metal
grey screen.

I remember.
I know how it's done.

You pull it down
real hard
and take advantage
of the
weight of the world
on your shoulders.

You look up to the hills
and spot the cathedral
highlighted in orange.

You take a breath
of fresh air,
you thank St. George for slaying the dragon
and remember the first time
you ever smoked a cigarette.

Pomeriggio

The sun seems a little nicer this afternoon.
Not as much attitude.
Cafe seats face the sidewalk,
face other faces.
They tell too many stories
or sometimes not enough.

A glass of water accompanies everything,
including an espresso ghiacciato,
and this air makes me sit up straight,
cross my legs,
hold the small cup delicate,
and sip with the fear of undeserved decadence.

The plan for tonight is simple:
"Io mi metto in Piazza e tu mi venga a trovare."
That's where gossip begins:
prima di internet,
prima di cell phones,
before the excuses to stay home.

It was sitting on vespas,
cracking the loudest battuta
with dressed style of modest elegance.
Who could use the most poetic
combination of parolace:
employ subtle peripherals on
the bella donna with olive skin.

A shadow I don't quite see walks by
"Non guardare"
before swallows,
then makes the sign of the cross
looking over your shoulder

for Cyrano or Quasimodo—nowhere

to be found,
you romance the romance language.
"Buona sera."

Blood Orange Sun

I miss seeing you
look over your shoulder,
and give us a playful but sorrowful glance
before ducking yourself down
and saying goodbye.

I miss the feeling of citrus spray
at dusk reminding us
that we're rested,
that we need to tuck in our shirts,
leave the first two buttons undone,
show a little more leg
and rub our wrists together
with perfume and cologne.

"Buona sera, ma quanto siamo elegante."

Blood orange sun—
ombrelones on the beach close,
surrounded by the day's enthusiastic footprints.

The clouds sufficiently flirt,
still warm
with that pink tinge of curious desire,
and by example,
I put the same rose between my teeth.

"Sta sera balliamo"

Blood orange sun—
we're in the salad you tossed,
that field between motion
and emotion,
between what we say

and how we sway.
Stepping with red wine wisdom,
our eyes delicate in this receding rhythm,
my hand touches what I believe
to be your hip,
solemnly navigates black fibres
finds the same shade of night
in your dress that will eventually
cradle and surrender
a blood orange afterglow.

Variations in the Sea

My brother
has decided
to become a monk,

to leave behind
the sixteen year old
hot shot
who had Modicano girls
unable to keep
their eyes off him.
At twenty,
he has decided
to grow his beard
and devote his life
to an order of monks
that has existed
in Sicily for centuries.

That night
my Dad
came to visit me
in my dreams.
He chose the setting himself,
the beach with the burned down factory
on the cliffs where he used
to take me as a child.

Deserted silence
surrounded us
and untouched smooth sand
lay under our feet,
He looked at me
and said, "What gives?"

And I said, Dad,
it looks like
we've switched roles here.
I always used to ask you
for answers,
like when we drove
over the Guerrieri bridge,
and I'd ask why there
were flowers on the rails,
and you'd waste no time
telling me it was because
people jumped.

Or when I asked you
about the burned down factory,
you wasted no time,
telling me it was bombed
in the war.

And you even had answers
for the sea,

I remember driving in the car
and when we'd first
glimpse the sea from
a distance,
you'd be able to
tell me if the water
was calm, or fierce.

You said, if there were variations
in the sea, it would be calm,
but if it was a solid blue
the water would be choppy,

like it is right now
as the roaring waves
try to drown us out.
And again you ask me,

"What gives?"

And I say, Dad,
how should I know?
You made your ascension early,
leaving me with a whole host
of unanswered questions,
but I'll answer you anyway.

I'll tell you that
I envied my brother
when I met him again
after eight years.
I envied the 16 year old
hot shot,
who had girls looking him
up and down,
and his whole life ahead
of him,
because his slate
was far cleaner than mine.
And now,
I envy him even more,
because he dove into his faith
so hard,
that he decided to stick around,
and whenever I dive into mine,
I'm told that
I'm not doing it right

or I trip over obstacles
that weren't there before.

But maybe, Dad,
he's doing it
because he hears your echo still,
because you left him
with more unanswered questions
than me.

Maybe he's doing it,
because I haven't been
the greatest brother,
and I want to call him
brother,
and he wants to be called
"brother."

Maybe he's doing it
because we both look through
the same coloured glasses.
We thought you were
stronger than Superman,
and seeing you,
with your eyes closed
in a coffin,
just hasn't sunk in
like it's supposed to.

We both wanted
different lives with you,
but they both involved
pictures with smiles,
that we could look

back on and say,
"That was a great time."

My Dad stood silent.
He offered his hand
and I took it.
We soared through air
and landed on a hilltop.
He came around me,
put his hands
on my shoulders.
I closed my eyes
when he took them off.
I turned around,
he was gone,
nowhere to be found,
and when I turned
in the other direction,
from a distance
I saw
variations in the sea.

Queen Street East

"You wanted me to see what I had planted…"

Jigsaw

On my walk tonight
I entered a fragment in time.
Summer 1997:
Timothy McVeigh sentenced to death,
Che Guevara's remains sent back to Cuba,
and the movie Boogie Nights
was the Saturday Night Fever
of my time.
A July night with still humidity,
an occasional breeze
a blessing.
I finished work at 3 a.m.
smelling like a restaurant kitchen.
The Beaches ended its
death rattle,
after new town houses
on the track
and before we stopped knowing
a place called Sirens.
Dad dying felt like
it was yesterday.
At 21 I numbed the pain
by giving God
and everyone else the finger.
Friday night.
The Sunset Grill
stayed open 24 hours.
Tom ordered a BLT,
I had scrambled eggs.
We crossed the street
to Kew Gardens
and sat on the steps
of the gazebo.
Clubbers had the same idea

and teenagers scattered
for make-out sessions.
While Tom rolled one,
we talked about which waitress
from work we'd ask out.
Tom said he'd go for Kelly,
'cause she's an LA beach blonde,
avocados, waves, and surfs up .
I said I'd ask out Braeda
'cause she liked incense
and was into Tori Amos.
Cess lingered.
We reminisced,
laughed at how
one of the owners
got into his Corvette,
rolled his windows down,
and blared Rick Springfield
at 2:00 in the morning.

Which one of us
was the true Cruisin USA champion?
We were gonna rule the world.
I was gonna do it from
the stage and screen,
and Tom was gonna do it
from one of the many buildings
he'd build.
It was before
the press chased Diana
through a tunnel leading
to oblivion,
and before we asked the question
What is the Matrix?

The Millenium was on its way
and we were sure
there would never be
any flies on us,
business would always
be booming,
it was always gonna be
a peaceful world.
Checking my heart rate,
I looked at the Sunset Grill,
it had been closed
since 4 p.m.
At the gazebo,
three kids
failed at skateboarding.
No one sat on the steps.
Those days
were a jigsaw puzzle,
the kind
where you'd throw
the pieces in the air,
sure they'd fall on the table
intact,
and didn't care
what the picture was

Anybody Seen Jimi?

Why did they take Jimi's picture down?

He wasn't hurting anybody.
He was just minding his own business,
keeping watch
over Leslieville,
picking at his guitar
while the wind cried Mary.
I passed it on the 501
daily,
heading westbound
into the thick of the smoke,
the cogs of the grind.

On that east wall
where that guitar shop used to be.
How many musicians
would say, "I bought it at that guitar shop
with Jimi on the wall,"
as they sat in their basements
showing off a shiny new Gibson.

Now that guitar shop is no more,
another domino falling
in the ever changing chameleon
we call a city.
Now it's a tea shop,
and where Jimi used to be,
is a psychedelic confusion.
How did they know
Jimi didn't like to sip
on an orange pekoe, or even
a chamomile after a show?

Next time I'm on the 501
heading westbound,
I'll keep my eyes in my book,
do my best not to look up
just before Leslie,
I'll try not to mourn
you, Jimi.

Know your vibe
is still reverberating
within these confines,
smiling down upon
those good natured
merchants who go by *Mom and Pop*,
staving off attacks
from the big box stores,
keeping people
with tipsy heads
and full bellies
in funky restaurants,
and helping them
rise to greet a good morning,
in Tango Palaces.

So long Jimi.
Glad it wasn't a wrecking ball.
I could have stopped it if
I had some of that voodoo,
but no such luck.
I'll be strong.
You'll see me turn into a beast.
I'll be standing next to a mountain.

This Whistleblower

Waiting for the subway,
a guy with sunglasses comes to me and randomly starts talking.
He blows alcohol with every breath
and says he's from Ireland.
He tells me
that there will be
thirty hours of thunderstorms.
On the opposing eastbound platform,
a train is about to close its doors
when the chimes sound.
He smiles at me
reaches into his shirt pocket
and pulls out a whistle.
"This is what I used to use when I worked for them," he says.
To humour him
I say "Back when they used to be red right?"
He nods his head
and laughs.
I remember those trains
as a kid and how the lights used to go off in the tunnel.

It would be
three eternal seconds of horror.
I picture him
dressed in a dingy TTC uniform
using that darkness time
to take a swig
of Maker's Mark,
leaving him
with just enough strength
to blow the whistle at Ossington Station.
He gets off early at Broadview station
puts his hands on my shoulder
as he exits the car

and says "take care."
I nod my head to him.
Over the Bloor via-duct
I see the northbound DVP
clogged with traffic to eternity
and a giant blackish grey cloud
blanketing the cityscape
supposedly containing
thirty hours-worth of storms.

Sky Writing

For Nik Beat

How do you write a tribute in the sky
when there are only so many characters?

On a grey windy day
in the fall, I saw
a lone gentleman
wearing a black leather vest,
his many crosses around his neck
catching the wind.
He stood with his hands
in his pockets
on Queen Street East
by the stone wall
taking one last look.

How do you write an ode
in the midst of stars?
Be creative,
make your way around the dark.

And this is how you stand on your own,
encased in an eternal glimmer
with the most magnificent pen.
And this is how you give the finger,
making no apologies for the trail
of fire and pixie dust
you leave behind.
Sniff it out and follow
with your own inventive steps.

And this is how you howl
in your playground of night
brewing the storm with fangs,

painting black eyeliner,
and opening the gothic calamity
with the chain link
of reinforced lexicon
over and over again.

And this is how you love
in a parked car with fogged windows
by a graveyard,
in a field of daisies
under the intense midday sun of lust,
in a drunk and stoned haze of afterglow,
and long hair,
and clasped hands,
and the sweet sinking.

And this is how you meet God
with an attitude,
telling him the ego has landed,
ready to show him
your Irish boxing moves.
and him asking you
if you've changed your mind.
And this is my tribute in the sky.

And this is how I picture you,
on an early afternoon,
in Cartoon Rome,
sitting at a table
sipping a Diet Coke.
You observe a young man
and young woman
studying romantic science

against a stone wall.
The Trevi Fountain
sprinkles psychedelic.
And this is how I close my eyes and see you,
forever etched and embossed.
And this is how you nudge me forward.
This is how I pass it on.
This is how I whisper my cries,
This is how I write goodbye
in the sky.

The Sower

For Norman Cristofoli

You told me to come by,
look at the sunflowers.
You wanted me
to see what I'd planted—
seven feet tall, you said.
I needed to see it for myself.
Your incubated garden—
the backyard,
the small relationship I had
with Sunflowers.
They're still my favourites—
obvious personalities
always in good moods.

I remember that day,
followed it,
glided on its timeline
of how things should have unfolded.
You hobbled—
perhaps it was an overdose
or over exertion
of passion.

I carried the heavy bags
of soil to the backyard.
You taught me
how to spread the earth evenly,
how deep to dig,
and how delicately
to let the seeds
fall from my hands.

Later,
we chewed through medium-well steak
and buttered potatoes,
and allowed ourselves
the luxury of profanity
in our conversation.
I left that night
to a walk on still air.

I levitated just above
my mattress,
kept fatigue at bay
and thought about
the relationships between
gardens, parents,
and their children.

My grandfather
held up his tomato plants
with broken hockey sticks
that I wanted to use.
I'd run from my Mom
at the first mention of gardening—
Vito Corleone died in the garden
while playing with his grandson.
In the Garden of Gethsemane,
Jesus knew he was out of options,
obeyed his father,
and followed the passion of prophecy.

Tonight,
while looking at the pictures
of the sunflowers,

I reflect
on your ability
to cross realms
and enter other dimensions.
I know it's not
so easily accessible,
that it's a lost symbol
or tongued spell
that opens that door.
I picture you there,
playing possum with Buddha,
flirting with truth,
and waiting for the wind
to blow the Sorceress'
robes open.

Somewhere in those confines
is the garden untouched
by the seeds my Father and I
never sowed—
but there is a trail
of footprints visible.
I know there was a time
when God took you by the hand,
showed you how to spread
the earth evenly,
how deep to dig,
and how delicately
to let the seeds
fall from your hands.
It came in the form of
ink droplets,
and precious virgin thoughts.

When the telescope
points in the other direction,
God will show you
how you connected
the celestial dots in your sleep
and present you with
one of your very own.
A mirror in the sky
will appear
when you reach
that certain altitude,
and his voice will come to you—
he'll tell you
that you have to see it for yourself.
He'll take you by the hand
and show you
what you planted.

Valentino Assenza has been a published poet and spoken word artist for over two decades. He has publIshed four chapbooks of poetry: *Wandering Absence*, *Il Ritorno* (Labour Of Love Productions), *Quiet Confessions of a Loudmouth* and *Make Our Peace With Rattlesnakes* (Lyricalmyrical Press). He has had numerous pieces of poetry published in anthologies such as *Labour Of Love* and *Descant* Magazine. He has read and performed his poetry throughout Canada and the U.S.A. Valentino was a member of the Toronto Poetry Slam team in 2009 and 2010 and has performed his poetry at the Canadian Festival of Spoken Word and The National Poetry Slam. Valentino sat on the committees for the Art Bar Poetry Series and Toronto Poetry Project. He currently lives in Toronto, and is the co-host and co-producer of Howl, a spoken word, literary radio show, Tuesday nights at 10pm on CIUT 89.5 FM.

www.ingramcontent.com/pod-product-compliance
Lightning Source LLC
Chambersburg PA
CBHW071730090426
42738CB00011B/2447